# WARREN BUFFETT

## The Life, Lessons & Rules For Success

## Philosophers Notes

**Philosophers Notes**

# CONTENTS

# LIFE

Warren Buffett is an American businessman, investor, and philanthropist. He is widely considered to be one of the most successful investors in history, and is currently the chairman and largest shareholder of Berkshire Hathaway, a multinational conglomerate holding company.

Buffett was born in Omaha, Nebraska in 1930. He showed an early interest in business and investing, and by the age of 11, he had already purchased his first stock. He attended the University of Nebraska and later received a master's degree in economics from Columbia University.

In the early years of his career, Buffett worked as a stockbroker and investment salesman. In 1962, he formed Berkshire Hathaway, which initially focused on textile manufacturing. However, Buffett soon shifted the company's focus to insurance and investment, and it has since grown to become one of the largest and most profitable companies in the world.

Buffett's investment strategies are known for their long-term approach, and he has become famous for his ability to identify undervalued companies and turn them into highly profitable investments. He is also known for his frugal lifestyle, and for his commitment to giving away the majority of his wealth to charity.

In addition to his business career, Buffett is also a well-known philanthropist. He and Bill Gates founded The Giving Pledge, an initiative that encourages the world's wealthiest individuals to donate the majority of their wealth to charity. He has also made large donations to organizations such as the Gates Foundation, the Susan G. Komen Breast Cancer Foundation, and the Howard G. Buffett Foundation, which focuses on reducing poverty and hunger.

Buffett is considered to be one of the most successful investors in history, and is often referred to as the "Oracle of Omaha" for his ability to predict market trends and make highly profitable investments. His net worth is estimated to be around $110 billion as of 2021, making him one of the wealthiest people in the world.

# IDEAS

## *Invest in what you understand.*

Warren Buffett, widely considered as one of the most successful investors in history, has always emphasized the importance of investing in what you understand. One example of this is his investment in Coca-Cola. Buffett has been a long-time investor in the company and has said that he can understand the company's business model and its competitive advantages in the market. He has said that he can predict the company's future earnings and therefore, he can predict the future value of the company.

Another example is his investment in American Express. Buffett invested in American Express during the 1960s when the company was facing a crisis due to a scandal. He understood the company's business model and believed that the company had a strong brand and a loyal customer base. He believed that the company would recover from the scandal and that the stock was undervalued. His investment turned out to be a wise decision and American Express became one of Berkshire Hathaway's (the company owned by Warren Buffett) most successful investments. By investing in companies and industries that he understands, Buffett has been able to make informed decisions and increase his chances of making successful investments. This is why he advises others to do the same.

## *Be patient.*

Warren Buffett is known for his long-term investment strategy and his ability to be patient. One example of this is his investment in Coca-Cola. Buffett first invested in the company in 1988 and has held on to his shares since then. He has said that he believes in the company's long-term potential and has no plans to sell his shares. He has also said that he believes in the company's brand and its ability to generate consistent earnings. His patience with this investment has paid off as Coca-Cola has been one of Berkshire Hathaway's (the company owned by Warren Buffett) most successful investments.

Another example is his investment in Wells Fargo, he first invested in the company in 1989 and held on to his shares even during the 2008 financial crisis, when many investors panicked and sold their shares. His patience paid off as the company recovered from the crisis and the value of his investment increased.

By being patient and investing for the long-term, Buffett has been able to increase his chances of success and avoid the pitfalls of trying to make quick gains. This is why he advises others to adopt the same approach.

## *Be disciplined.*

Warren Buffett is known for his discipline in sticking to his investment strategy, even when the market is volatile. One example of this is his investment in Berkshire Hathaway. When he first took over the company in 1965, the market was in a bearish phase and many investors were selling their stocks. But Buffett held on to his shares and invested in companies that he believed in, even when the market was down. His discipline paid off as Berkshire Hathaway's stock price has risen significantly since then.

Another example is during the 2008 financial crisis, when many investors panicked and sold their stocks, Buffett remained disciplined and stuck to his investment strategy. He continued to invest in companies that he believed in and even used the opportunity to buy more shares of companies that he believed were undervalued. His discipline helped him to take advantage of the market downturn and make profitable investments.

By being disciplined and sticking to his investment strategy, even in volatile market conditions, Buffett has been able to achieve long-term success. He advises others to adopt the same approach, to avoid the pitfalls of trying to time the market or react to short-term market fluctuations.

## *Live below your means.*

Warren Buffett is known for his frugal lifestyle and his ability to live below his means. He has said that he does not believe in living an extravagant lifestyle and that he is content with living a simple life. One example of this is his home, Buffett has lived in the same modest house in Omaha, Nebraska since 1958, even though he could afford a much more luxurious home. He has said that he sees no need for a larger home and that his current home is more than enough for him.

Another example is his car, Buffett is known to have driven an old Cadillac for many years and he has said that he sees no need to buy a new car, as long as his current car is running well.

By living below his means, Buffett has been able to save and invest a significant amount of his income, which has allowed him to achieve financial freedom and invest in his future. He advises others to do the same and to avoid the trap of living beyond their means.

# *Be honest.*

Warren Buffett is known for his integrity and honesty. He places great value on building trust and strong relationships, and believes that honesty is essential for achieving this. One example of this is his approach to business, Buffett has always been transparent in his business dealings, he always communicates openly and honestly with his shareholders, partners and employees. He believes that this honesty is key to building trust and strong relationships with his stakeholders.

Another example is in his philanthropy, Buffett has always been transparent and honest about his philanthropic efforts. He has been open about the causes he supports, the organizations he donates to, and the amount of money he donates. He believes that this honesty is key to building trust and strong relationships with the organizations and communities he supports.

By being honest, Buffett has been able to build trust and strong relationships with his stakeholders. He advises others to do the same and to avoid the pitfalls of dishonesty and deceit.

## *Learn from your mistakes.*

Warren Buffett has made mistakes in the past, but he has always believed in learning from them and moving on. One example of this is his investment in Berkshire Hathaway's textile division. In the 1960s, Buffett invested heavily in the textile division and it was a major part of Berkshire Hathaway's operations. However, the division was not profitable and it was clear that it was not going to be a viable business in the long run. Rather than continuing to pour money into the division, Buffett closed it down in 1985, he admits this was a mistake but he learned from it and moved on.

Another example is his investment in the company US Airways. In 1989, Buffett invested in the company's preferred stock, but he didn't do enough due diligence on the company and the investment ended up being a mistake. However, he learned from his mistake and did not repeat it again.

By learning from his mistakes, Buffett has been able to improve his investment strategy and avoid making the same mistakes in the future. He advises others to do the same and to not let past mistakes hold them back.

## *Give back.*

Warren Buffett is known for his philanthropy and his commitment to giving back to society. He has pledged to give away 99% of his wealth to charity during his lifetime or in his will. One example of this is his Giving Pledge, a commitment by some of the world's wealthiest individuals and families to give away the majority of their wealth to philanthropy. In 2010, he announced his intention to give away 99% of his wealth to charitable causes, and he has been true to his word.

Another example is his donation to the Bill and Melinda Gates Foundation, in 2010, he pledged to give away the bulk of his wealth to the foundation, which focuses on improving health and reducing poverty around the world. His donation was $31 billion, the largest charitable donation in history. He has also donated to a number of other organizations, including the Susan Thompson Buffett Foundation, which focuses on education and reproductive health.

By giving back, Buffett has been able to make a positive impact on society and help improve the lives of others. He advises others to do the same and to consider giving back to their communities and to causes they care about.

## *Read a lot.*

Warren Buffett is known to be an avid reader and he believes that reading is essential to gaining knowledge and making better decisions. He has said that he reads for about five to six hours a day, and he has been doing this for most of his life.

One example of this is when he was a kid, he would read books on investing and business and he would read annual reports of companies. This reading helped him to gain knowledge about different industries and companies, which in turn helped him to make better investment decisions. He has also been known to read books on history, economics and other subjects.

Another example is when he was asked about how he became a successful investor, he said "I just read and read and read. I read everything I could get my hands on. I read about investing, I read about business, I read about economics, I read about psychology, I read about history."

By reading a lot, Buffett has been able to gain knowledge and make better decisions. He advises others to do the same, and to read as much as possible to gain knowledge and to improve their decision-making skills.

# QUOTES

## *"Risk comes from not knowing what you're doing."*

"Risk comes from not knowing what you're doing" is a quote by Warren Buffett that highlights the importance of understanding the risks involved in any investment or decision-making. He believes that when you don't understand the risks involved in an investment, you're more likely to make a poor decision that can lead to financial losses.

For example, Buffett is known for investing in companies that he knows well and has a deep understanding of their industry and business model. He avoids investing in companies or industries that he doesn't understand because he believes that the risk of making a poor investment is too high.

In 2008, when the global financial crisis hit, many investors were losing money as the market was crashing. Buffett, on the other hand, was able to avoid large losses because he understood the risks and avoided investing in companies that were highly leveraged or had complex financial products. He knew that these companies were more likely to fail during a market downturn, and he avoided them.

Therefore, the quote highlights the importance of understanding the risks involved in any investment or decision-making, and how it can help to avoid financial losses. It suggests that it is better to not invest in something if you don't have the knowledge and understanding of it, rather than investing blindly.

*"The stock market is a device
for transferring money from the
impatient to the patient."*

"The stock market is a device for transferring money from the impatient to the patient" is a quote by Warren Buffett that highlights the importance of patience in investing in the stock market. He believes that the stock market rewards those who are patient and disciplined in their investment strategy.

For example, Buffett is known for his long-term investment strategy. He does not focus on short-term fluctuations in the market, but instead looks for undervalued companies with strong fundamentals that he believes will perform well over the long-term. He will often hold onto these investments for years or even decades, waiting for the market to recognize the value of these companies.

In contrast, many investors are impatient and try to make quick gains by buying and selling stocks based on short-term market fluctuations. This approach often leads to poor investment decisions and financial losses.

Therefore, the quote highlights the importance of patience in investing in the stock market and how it can lead to better investment decisions and long-term success. It suggests that those who are patient and disciplined in their investment strategy are more likely to be successful in the stock market, and those who are impatient are more likely to lose money.

## *"Price is what you pay. Value is what you get."*

"Price is what you pay. Value is what you get" is a quote by Warren Buffett that highlights the importance of understanding the difference between price and value when investing. He believes that the price of an investment should not be the only consideration, but rather the underlying value of the investment should be taken into account.

For example, when looking to invest in a company, Buffett looks beyond the current stock price and focuses on the company's fundamentals such as its financials, management, and competitive position in the market. He looks for companies that he believes are undervalued based on these fundamentals, even if the stock price is currently low.

In contrast, many investors focus solely on the stock price and buy stocks that have recently gone up in value without considering the underlying value of the company. This approach often leads to overpaying for a stock and can lead to poor investment decisions.

Therefore, the quote highlights the importance of understanding the difference between price and value when investing. It suggests that investors should focus on the underlying value of an investment rather than the current stock price in order to make better investment decisions.

*"It takes 20 years to build
a reputation and five
minutes to ruin it."*

"It takes 20 years to build a reputation and five minutes to ruin it" is a quote by Warren Buffett that highlights the importance of maintaining a positive reputation. He believes that it takes a significant amount of time and effort to build a good reputation, but that one bad decision or action can cause irreparable damage in a very short amount of time.

For example, Buffett is known for his commitment to maintaining a strong reputation for integrity and honesty. Throughout his career, he has carefully cultivated a reputation as a reliable and trustworthy businessman. This reputation has helped him to build successful business partnerships and to attract loyal investors.

On the other hand, a company that has a history of unethical practices, such as insider trading or accounting fraud, will find it difficult to regain trust and credibility with the public, even if they make efforts to improve. This will make it harder to attract new investors, customers and suppliers which can have a negative impact on the company's financial performance.

Therefore, the quote highlights the importance of being mindful of the actions that can damage a reputation and being careful to maintain a good one. It suggests that it is important to be aware of the long-term consequences of one's actions and to be mindful of the effect they may have on one's reputation.

*"The best investment you can make is in your own abilities. Anything you can do to develop your own abilities is likely to be more productive than any other investment you can make."*

"The best investment you can make is in your own abilities" is a quote by Warren Buffett that emphasizes the importance of investing in oneself. He believes that the most valuable investment one can make is in developing and improving one's own abilities, as it will lead to greater success in all aspects of life.

For example, Buffett is known for being a voracious reader and learner, who spends much of his time reading and studying various subjects, including business, economics, and history. He also encourages others to read and learn as much as they can. He believes that reading and learning provide a strong foundation for making informed decisions and for understanding the world around us.

Another example is the way he invested in his abilities as an investor, he started reading annual reports of different companies at the age of 11, and by the time he was 14, he had already bought his first stock. Through consistent learning and practice, he has become one of the most successful investors in history.

Therefore, the quote highlights the importance of continuously investing in one's own abilities, whether it be through education, training, or personal development. It suggests that by investing in oneself, one can improve their chances of success in any field.

> *"It's far better to buy a wonderful company at a fair price than a fair company at a wonderful price."*

"It's far better to buy a wonderful company at a fair price than a fair company at a wonderful price." is a quote by Warren Buffett that emphasizes the importance of investing in companies with strong fundamentals and long-term growth potential. He believes that investing in such companies will provide greater returns in the long run, even if they may be slightly more expensive in the short term.

For example, one of Buffett's most famous investments is in Coca-Cola. In 1988, he invested $1 billion in the company, despite the fact that the stock was trading at a premium. He believed that Coca-Cola had a strong brand, a wide moat, and long-term growth potential. Today, that investment is worth over $16 billion, and Berkshire Hathaway continues to hold a significant stake in the company.

Another example is when Berkshire Hathaway invested in Apple Inc. in 2016, it was trading at a P/E ratio of just 10 and a P/B ratio of just 3, but Buffett believed that Apple was a wonderful company with a strong brand, a wide moat, and long-term growth potential. Today, that investment is worth over $120 billion.

Therefore, the quote highlights the importance of investing in companies with strong fundamentals and long-term growth potential, rather than focusing solely on the price. It suggests that by investing in such companies, one can achieve greater returns in the long run.

*"I always knew I was going to be rich. I don't think I ever doubted it for a minute."*

This quote from Warren Buffett highlights his self-confidence and belief in his own abilities. He believes that having a strong sense of self-belief and knowing that you are capable of achieving success is important in order to achieve it. An example of this can be seen in his career, where he has consistently made successful investments and built a reputation as one of the most successful investors in history. Despite facing challenges and setbacks, he never doubted his ability to achieve his goals. For example, at the age of 11, he bought his first stock and by the time he was 14, he had saved $5,000 from delivering newspapers, selling golf balls and stamps, and doing odd jobs. His belief in his ability to become rich helped him to continue making wise investments and building his wealth.

*"The most important investment
you can make is in yourself."*

This quote from Warren Buffett emphasizes the importance of investing in oneself. He believes that investing in one's own abilities, education, and personal growth is more important than any other type of investment. An example of this can be seen in his own life, where he has consistently invested in his own education and development. For example, He spent hours reading and studying business, investing and economics. He also took a job at a local brokerage firm to learn more about the stock market and investing. He also took a job as a salesperson at a department store to learn more about how businesses operate and how to sell products to customers. By investing in himself and his own abilities, he was able to become a successful investor and build a reputation as one of the most successful investors in history.

*"I never attempt to make money on the stock market. I buy on the assumption that they could close the market the next day and not reopen it for five years."*

Warren Buffett's quote highlights his long-term investment approach. He believes that it is more important to focus on the value and potential of a company rather than trying to make quick gains on the stock market. He also believes in investing in companies that have a strong track record, and that have the potential to perform well in the long run, even if the market conditions are difficult. An example of this approach is when he invested in Coca-Cola in the 1980s, he knew that the company had a strong brand and a track record of consistent growth, so he invested in the company even though the market conditions were difficult at the time. This investment turned out to be a wise decision, as Coca-Cola's stock value has grown significantly over the years.

*"You only have to do a very few
things right in your life so long as you
don't do too many things wrong."*

This quote by Warren Buffett emphasizes the importance of making smart and calculated decisions, rather than trying to do too much and potentially making mistakes. For example, an investor may choose to only invest in a few select companies that they have thoroughly researched and understand, rather than spreading their money across multiple companies and industries that they may not be as familiar with. By focusing on a few key investments, the investor is more likely to make profitable decisions and avoid costly mistakes. Similarly, a business owner may choose to only focus on a few key products or services, rather than trying to offer a wide range, in order to maximize their chances of success.

# ABOUT THE AUTHOR

## Philosophers Notes

 At Philosophers Notes, we strive to gain insight and inspiration from some of the world's most accomplished individuals. By examining their journeys, we can gain a deeper understanding of the challenges and triumphs that shape their paths to success. We aim to share their stories, highlighting key principles and valuable lessons that can be applied to our own lives in order to achieve great results.

Printed in Great Britain
by Amazon

37129918R00020